92
PAT
Peifer, Charles
Soldier of destiny

$11.95

DATE			

19460

D1295817

19460

SOLDIER OF DESTINY

A People in Focus Book

Soldier of Destiny

A BIOGRAPHY OF GEORGE PATTON

CHARLES PEIFER, JR.

Ð | DILLON PRESS, INC.
Minneapolis, Minnesota 55415

To Chuckie, my favorite wise guy

Acknowledgments

Photographs have been reproduced through the courtesy of the Eisenhower Library; the Huntington Library, San Marino, California; the George C. Marshall Foundation; the National Archives; the Patton Museum (David A. Holt); the United States Army; the United States Military Academy at West Point; and the Virginia Military Institute. Special thanks go to Helen for her help and support.

Library of Congress Cataloging-in-Publication Data

Peifer, Charles.
Soldier of destiny : a biography of George Patton / by Charles Peifer, Jr.

(People in focus)
Bibliography: p.
Includes index.
Summary: A biography of General George S. Patton, covering his life and career in the U.S. Army through both World Wars.
ISBN 0-87518-395-6

1. Patton, George S. (George Smith), 1885-1945—Juvenile literature. 2. Generals—United States—Biography—Juvenile literature. 3. United States. Army—Biography—Juvenile literature. 4. United States—History, Military—20th century—Juvenile literature. [1. Patton, George S. (George Smith) 1885-1945. 2. Generals.]   I. Title. II. Series: People in focus book.
E745.P3P39   1989
355'.0092'4—dc 19
[B]
[92]   88-20265
                                                           CIP
                                                           AC

Dillon Press, Inc., 242 Portland Avenue South
Minneapolis, Minnesota 55415

Printed in the United States of America
1 2 3 4 5 6 7 8 9 10 98 97 96 95 94 93 92 91 90 89

Contents

Chapter/One

The Happiest Boy in the World

Under his breath, not knowing Papa would hear, little Georgie Patton called himself "George S. Patton, Jr., Lieutenant General." Papa, wanting to encourage his son's interest in the military, bought Georgie a colorful soldier suit, complete with a sword and a bolt-action rifle. As father and son took walks together, Georgie would pretend to shoot at lions and robbers and would slash the tops off of cactus plants with gusto.

Even at an early age, George Patton knew exactly what he wanted to do with his life. A model soldier, George stood at attention and saluted Papa every morning. His dramatic flair would later enhance his image as a fighting general—commanding both admiration and fear.

Seven-year-old Georgie Patton poses in a sailor suit in 1892.

World War II, George Patton's ultimate test, proved his worth to the U.S. Army and to his country. He rose to command on the battlefield, brandishing the four stars of a full general on his shoulders. He fought his battles with enthusiasm and courage, ordering his men to advance into enemy lines with speed and power. Soldiers called General Patton "Old Blood and Guts," but after the war those same men proudly boasted, "I rolled with Patton."

George Smith Patton, Jr., was born on November 11, 1885, when the memory of the Civil War was still vivid in the nation's mind and industrialization steamed full speed across America. The inventions of machines and increasing numbers of factories had attracted many people to the cities for jobs, but California's small, dusty frontier towns still reflected the spirit of the Wild West and the days of the gold rush. Mining towns, cattle ranches, and good farmland continued to bring new settlers to the West.

The Patton family lived in a ranch house at the foot of the San Gabriel Mountains, overlooking Lake Vineyard. Shortly after George was born, the Pattons moved to Los Angeles, California, so that Papa could be closer to his work as district attorney

A portrait of George and Nita Patton and their mother, Ruth Wilson Patton.

of Los Angeles County. The family visited the ranch often, though, and George spent many days in the country.

George grew up surrounded by loving parents, his Aunt Nannie, servants, horses, and pets—including two dogs named Lancelot and Remus. His father taught him how to ride a horse, shoot a rifle, fish, hunt, sail, and fence. According to George, he was the "happiest boy in the world."

Papa spent many hours with his son and his daughter Anne—nicknamed Nita. George's education was unusual compared to that of other children his age. In the evenings, George and Nita would sit listening to Papa read aloud in a big overstuffed chair near the fireplace in the parlor. They took turns sitting in Papa's lap.

Papa read aloud mostly for George, who could not read or write. Letters seemed upside down or reversed to him. Today, medical professionals call this problem "dyslexia."

At the time, doctors knew little about George's learning disability, and his parents could not understand the problem completely. Still, they learned to be patient and loving and encouraged him to work hard. They also protected their son's pride by keeping him home from school where he might have been ridiculed by other students.

For eleven years, George learned at Papa's feet in spite of his dyslexia. He listened to stories of the great military men of history and literature, stories which his father chose with care. He learned about human struggles from the heroic adventures in Homer's *Iliad* and *Odyssey* and from William Shakespeare's plays. Soon, George had memorized long verses of poetry, and passages from Shakespeare, Rudyard Kipling, and the Bible. George's favorite stories were Sir Walter Scott's epics of life in Scotland. These exciting tales of bravery and romance instilled pride in his Scottish background.

George's father often talked to his son about

George Patton, at age ten.

the Patton family heritage. He explained to young
George that he had come from courageous ancestors who had first fought for Scotland, and then for
America in the Revolutionary War and the Civil
War. Stories of Grandfather Patton, who had been
killed in the Civil War, inspired George. He was
enchanted with the idea of being in the military, and
became convinced that he had lived before as a true
warrior, fearlessly conquering his enemies. George
vowed that he would not disappoint his ancestors—
especially not his grandfather.

From the time when the first Patton arrived in
Virginia, the male Pattons were established as
"southern gentlemen." Young George understood
that he was expected to uphold the tradition
proudly.

George's father had graduated from the Virginia Military Institute, as had his own father before
him. He then journeyed to California to study law.
There he met and married Ruth Wilson, George's
mother. Although his mother's side of the family
was wealthy and successful, George never took
much interest in the Wilsons. He was more interest-
ed in the aristocratic Pattons and the noble blood of
the southern gentleman.

When George was almost twelve, his parents
decided that their son was ready to go to school.

Down the Pasadena mule-car trolley line at Stephen Cutter Clark's School for Boys, George would take classes with other students from the best families in southern California.

Since George grew up listening to historical tales, history became his best subject. He spent hours reading about the great leaders and studying their personal qualities. In class reports, he wrote about Persian, Greek, and Roman generals, battle formations, and medieval wars. Themes of fame, glory, and heroism filled his papers.

Reading and writing, however, were still a struggle for George. He had to prod himself to concentrate. As his parents had feared, George's classmates laughed at his mistakes at the blackboard and mocked him when he read aloud. Yet criticism only inspired him to study harder, play harder, and throw himself into every activity with energetic, often reckless, determination. George learned that prizes in life were won by persistent effort.

George relished any opportunity to escape from school to be with his family. During summer vacations, the Patton family would board a steamboat from the San Pedro dock and sail to Santa Catalina Island, a resort for wealthy families. The island glistened with sandy beaches. Sleek sailing boats docked along its pier. Rugged mountains,

In 1900, the Patton family poses at Lake Vineyard in San Gabriel, California. Left to right: *George Patton, his mother, father, and sister.*

teeming with wild goats, offered excellent hunting.

George swam, sailed, fished for giant sea bass, and hunted goats with passion, energy, and determination. He wrote about one hunting trip when "a crowd gathered as usual and asked us how many goats we had killed. Each of the others had killed one while I had killed several, of which fact I boasted. Papa said, 'Son, it would have been more like a sportsman not to have mentioned the extra goats.'" George loved the attention—his character was taking shape.

While vacationing on the island in the summer of 1902, sixteen-year-old George met Beatrice Ban-

The Patton family, including Aunt Susie, Mr. Patton, George, Nita, and Mrs. Patton, gathers for dinner.

ning Ayer, a small, attractive girl from Boston, Massachusetts. He took a special interest in her when they acted together in a play for the adults. Beatrice, a refined and graceful girl who had been educated in European schools, played the lead role. George began to write letters to her after the Santa Catalina vacation, and she wrote back. Beatrice had made quite an impression on him, but that fall George had other things on his mind. He told Papa that he was ready to be a soldier.

Papa insisted that enlisting as a soldier in the army was out of the question. He wanted better things for his son, and felt that the only honorable

career in the army was as an officer. They both
agreed that the U.S. Military Academy at West
Point, in New York, would be the best place for
George to get the proper training.

Taking charge, Papa wrote the superintendent
of West Point, asking for the admission require-
ments. He quickly realized that it was not going to
be easy to get George accepted into the academy.
Although the Patton family connections were good,
he would still have to pass a written examination.
Papa worried that George's terrible spelling and his
difficulty with reading would stand in his way.

In addition to a passing score on the entrance
exam, West Point required that each candidate be
appointed by a government official. The academy
told George's father that his son's best chance for an
appointment was through Senator Thomas R. Bard
of California. His candidate at West Point would be
graduating the following year and the senator would
be ready to choose a new one.

George's father wrote to Senator Bard, and
asked many of his influential friends to recom-
mend his son for the appointment. Letters from
judges, lawyers, and prominent businessmen flooded Bard's office. Some focused on George's physical
qualifications; one doctor certified him to be six feet
tall, 165 pounds, with good eyes, strong teeth, and

sound hearing. Bard eventually agreed to consider George as a West Point candidate. First, though, George would have to pass the senator's own exam—a test that he gave to help him decide who to nominate for West Point.

Although George could not avoid Bard's test, Papa soon learned that his son could bypass the dreaded West Point examination. The academy would accept a certificate from a respected college in place of a test. Papa felt sure that he could get his son into the Virginia Military Institute. After all, attending VMI was a Patton tradition.

The family decided that George would spend a year at VMI. If he did not get Bard's appointment, he could still complete his course and enter the army.

As the time to report to VMI grew near, George grew nervous. He was worried that he might not be able to stand up to the rigorous studies or the strict discipline required for a military career. George was also concerned that he might not have the courage to be a soldier. When he confessed this concern to his Uncle Glassell Patton, his uncle told him that no Patton could be a coward. George's father reassured his son that although a Patton might be reluctant to get into a fist fight, he could "face death from weapons with a smile."

Finally, the day arrived for George to report for his first day at VMI. His father accompanied him. As George wrote, "When I had signed up, [the first captain] said, 'Of course you realize, Mr. Patton, that now your son is a cadet, he cannot leave the grounds.' Papa said, 'Of course.' "

Suddenly realizing he wouldn't be returning home with his family, George's spirits sank. "I never felt lower in my life," he wrote.

Chapter/Two

Good Soldier Blood

North of Lexington, Virginia, near the southern end of the historic and beautiful Shenandoah Valley, was the Virginia Military Institute. The gothic, fortresslike buildings stood on the outside border of a plateau, facing the parade ground that lay under the stern and constant gaze of Thomas "Stonewall" Jackson's statue.

George Patton was lost in a sea of fourth-class "rats," as new cadets were called. Swaggering third-classmen—themselves rats only the year before—cursed and shouted orders to the new cadets with smug arrogance. George learned to "brace," or to strike an exaggerated, uncomfortable pose of attention, in the presence of officers and upperclassmen. He endured the endless inspections when his cot

and locker were torn apart, even though everything was in its place.

Although he was nervous and uneasy at first, George's confidence returned when he discovered his uniform measurements were exactly the same as his father's and his grandfather's. He took this co-incidence as a good omen; it reinforced his belief that he was destined to become a soldier by some higher power.

On a visit to a nearby natural bridge with his mother, George noticed some girls showing interest in him and his sharp new uniform. One of the girls turned away in disgust, saying, "Oh, it's only a rat." George would not forget that the higher he climbed in the military, the more respect and attention he would earn.

Patton liked the discipline and routine of military life. Every day he had classes from eight o'clock until four, an hour of close order drill, and practice with the scrub football team. George performed his duties with careful attention to every detail.

The other VMI cadets liked George. In fact, he was the first rat at the institute to be accepted into a secret fraternity. George got along well with the other cadets, partly because they had also come from wealthy southern families. Patton began to feel that the military was an elite club.

George Patton, the "model soldier," wears his VMI uniform on the porch at Lake Vineyard in November 1903.

Before long, however, George's nagging dyslexia began to affect his schoolwork. Papa wrote
George to "keep at it till you work it out." George
followed his father's instructions and studied so
hard that by January, his grades ranked among the
highest in his class.

No matter how well he did at the institute,
success at VMI served only one purpose for
George: admission into the academy at West Point.
His letters to Papa were forever reminding him to
pressure Senator Bard, but George need not have
worried. On January 30, Papa sent word to George
that Bard's examination would be held in Los Angeles, on February 15, 1904.

Alarmed by the short notice, George hopped a
train for the six-day journey to California, and studied all along the way. Back with his family again, he
studied even harder. George and his father were
nervous wrecks until the examination ended.

George's hard work paid off. Senator Bard
nominated him for enrollment at West Point. The
next morning Papa wrote George a long letter ex-
pressing his relief. "It has been a long and tiresome
quest....You have in you good soldier blood....Be
honorable—brave—clean—and you will reap your
merited reward."

George was elated. All was proceeding as

George's official VMI portrait.

planned. He finished his year at VMI with excellent grades and a fresh feeling of confidence. The commandant even had plans to promote George to first corporal—the highest cadet appointment for second-year students—if he stayed at VMI. When George heard this, he knew that he had done well and that he could succeed at West Point, too.

During the American Revolution, George Washington had called West Point "the key to the continent." The land formed a plateau jutting out into the Hudson River. Washington had fortified the point, then stretched a gigantic chain across the river to keep the British from sailing up and cutting off New England from the rest of the colonies.

From then on, West Point was a permanent military post of the United States Army, named Fort Putnam. Years later, the United States Military Academy was established on West Point. When George Patton entered the academy in 1904, Fort Putnam still bristled with artillery batteries, aimed toward the Hudson highlands.

New cadets, called "plebes," began their first year at "plebe camp" as an introduction to military life. George wrote in a letter to his mother that "West Point is pretty nice....I have been treated a lot better than at VMI....they never touch you or swear."

George, however, was disappointed to discover that most of the other cadets seemed to lack the dedication and discipline that he believed were vital for the building of a soldier. He could not understand his classmates' laziness and their casual, easygoing attitudes. Patton set himself apart from the other cadets. He felt that he was in a "different class," and he was determined to outrank them all.

When classes started, George's learning problems came back to haunt him. He felt worthless and stupid. To George, failure was worse than death. He forced extra study on himself but no matter how hard he tried, he still remained in the middle of his class standings.

George often wrote to Papa to vent his feelings. "...I have always thought that I was a military genius or at least that I was or would be a great general.... [But] I see little in which to base such a belief. I am neither quicker nor brighter in any respect than other men, nor do they look upon me as a leader.... I have been trying my hardest for the last month... but to no purpose....It is disheartening and sickening to think that I am so stupid...though I study hard I don't go up while others who do not study... do well."

George also conveyed his frustrations to Beatrice Ayer. They had written to each other off and

on since George's VMI days, but now their letters
were more frequent. She seemed to understand
him, and responded to his letters with support and
encouragement.

In March 1905, George attended Theodore
Roosevelt's presidential inauguration. As a member
of the cadet corps, he marched in the parade
through the streets of Washington, D.C., reveling in
the roar of the crowds. Beatrice came, too, along
with her parents. George escorted her to the ball
that night, and they danced all evening. The young
cadet was coming down with a "bad attack of
puppy love."

By the end of the school year, George was do-
ing poorly in French and math. Failing grades usu-
ally meant dismissal from the academy, but the pro-
fessors recognized George's will to succeed. Because
they admired his snappy military nature and his
excellent performance in drill regulations, his pro-
fessors gave George another chance and allowed
him to repeat his first year at West Point.

When he returned to California for the summer, George's parents did not scold him for failing.
They offered their full love and support, encouraged him, and strengthened his confidence by hiring
a tutor to help him study for his next year at the
academy.

George traveled back east to spend a few days with Beatrice and her family before reporting to West Point. His attraction to her was growing, and he asked her "to every dance...from now until I graduate."

A few days before he returned to the academy, George bought a small notebook in which to record his thoughts. The first thing he wrote in it was "Do your damndest always."

Chapter/Three

Snap and Power

West Point was home to George once again. He breezed through plebe camp, and his classes were fairly easy for him at first. Soon, George ranked high in his class for military polish and stature. In his notebook, he scribbled important thoughts: "Do everything possible to attract attention.... Always be very neat; and when you get any new clothes, let every one know it. Do [everything] with all the snap and power you possess....When ordered to do a thing, carry out the spirit as well as the letter. Do all you *can*, not only all you *have* to do."

George practiced what he preached. At football games, he played with such reckless zeal that he finally landed in the hospital with a broken arm.

After that, he worked on his fencing and ran the high hurdles in track. George was determined to prove himself in every endeavor.

He pushed study habits almost beyond his limits, but his grades continued to be average. George, however, passed his classes, advanced into his second year, and was promoted to second corporal. His wishes had come true.

Corporal Patton now commanded a company of cadets, and was among the upperclassmen assigned to break in the plebes at summer camp. George tried as hard as he could to project a polished military image, and had certain ideas about how a military man should look and act. His uniform was always perfect, as was his posture. He wanted to assure his ancestors that he was carrying on the noble Patton heritage.

Wielding the power of authority, George's confidence returned. Corporal Patton commanded the plebes with military efficiency and discipline, and they hated him for it. He was a flawless soldier, determined to wrench the imperfections out of his men. His unbending attitude led him to hand out more demerits than any other officer.

George's superiors noticed how unpopular the young corporal was among the plebes, and they demoted him, lowering his rank to sixth corporal.

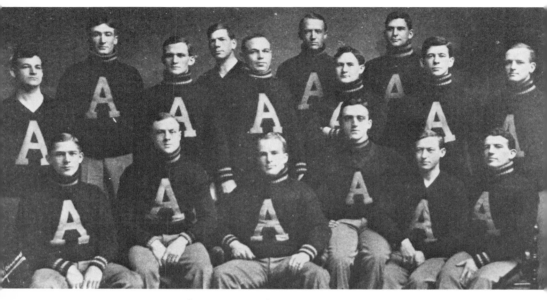

Varsity team members wearing the West Point A (for army) appear together. George Patton is second from the right in the back row.

"I was too damned military," George wrote to Bea.

Determined to prove himself, George went out for football once more. When injuries from playing too hard again forced him off the team, he turned to the broadsword, horsemanship, polo, and shooting. He qualified as an expert rifleman. George also did well in track, breaking a record for the 220-yard low hurdles, and won his army A.

George was so eager to test his bravery that he sometimes acted foolishly. One day on the rifle range, George was scoring targets in the pits while his classmates fired off rounds. Suddenly wondering if he would be afraid under fire, George stood up and stared down the blazing gun muzzles of the firing line as the bullets zipped and whizzed around him. He escaped the stunt unharmed, confident of his ability to keep his cool in the din of battle.

In the spring of his sophomore year, George was promoted to second corporal. The year after, he became a sergeant major, and then realized his greatest ambition when he was named adjutant (second in command) of the Corps of Cadets.

As executive officer, Lieutenant George S. Patton moved into the first captain's tower room in the First Division. Every morning, bracing rigidly in his gold braided uniform, he read the orders of the day from the center of the parade ground. As the corps marched in formation, George strutted proudly in the lead, thrilled by the attention focused on him.

In his spare time and on vacations, George visited Beatrice, and she came to dances and football games at West Point. During George's senior year, his affection for Beatrice blossomed into love. He had met other interesting girls, but, "Bea," as he called her, was the one for him. During Christmas vacation in 1908, George told Bea of his wish to marry her, but he didn't expect an immediate response. He wanted her to think about it before she gave him an answer.

As his senior year came to a close, George

Patton (left foreground) *at his graduation from West Point in 1909.*

began to think about which branch of the army he should enter as a second lieutenant. He narrowed down his choice to either the infantry, where soldiers fought on foot, or the cavalry, where troopers fought on horseback. Promotion was faster in the infantry, but the cavalry had horses and a better "class of gentlemen." George chose the cavalry.

On June 11, 1909, thick clouds rolled through the morning sky above the neatly trimmed West Point parade grounds. As army officials entered the academy's quarters, a seventeen-gun salute greeted them, and the Corps of Cadets marched in a parade. Graduation ceremonies had commenced.

George Patton, now twenty-four years old, graduated as number 46 in his class of 103 graduates.
His family witnessed the ritual, proud of their only
son, now an officer in the United States Army. A
captain told George's father that he should not wor-
ry about his son's future. "He always does more
than is asked of him," he said.

George spent a carefree summer in California
with his family before returning to the East, and
then went to visit Bea on his way to his first cavalry
assignment. One afternoon, as Bea lounged with her
family on the wide porch of their shoreside home
in Massachusetts, she heard a clattering of horse
hooves. A tall, slender officer mounted on horseback spurred his steed up the cut-stone steps and
onto the porch. Dismounting, the officer bowed
graciously at Bea's feet.

Lieutenant George S. Patton, Jr., had come to
call.

Chapter/Four

War Face

Lieutenant Patton entered the stable at his first duty station in Fort Sheridan, Illinois. Flies buzzed lazily around the horses as he strolled down the line of stalls, which were ready for his inspection. He found a horse untied.

Returning to his men, who were waiting nervously at the other end, he eyed the guilty soldier and scolded him for his carelessness. Patton instructed the soldier to run down to the stall, tie up the horse, then run back. He wanted to make the man look foolish in front of the other soldiers.

The man scurried off at a fast gait, but not a run.

"Run, damn you, run!" shouted Patton in his shrill voice.

The man bolted toward the horse, tied it up, and sprinted back.

Afterward, Patton gathered the men around and apologized to the soldier for insulting him by saying "damn you" instead of "damn it."

The men couldn't believe their ears—an officer apologizing to an enlisted man? Patton had long been known for his fiery tongue and his profane language. In fact, he cultivated this rough way of speaking because he believed it fit his warlike image. Apologizing to the soldier was a bitter pill for Patton to swallow, but he was glad he had done it.

The energetic young officer had a lot to learn about commanding soldiers. Patton felt that maintaining a tough outward appearance as a leader of men was essential for effective leadership. He would stand in front of a mirror scowling fiercely to develop a good "war face," the silent, grim expression he felt a warrior should display.

His rehearsals of the composed, confident officer proved valuable. One warm, dusty afternoon his horse threw its head back and cut Patton's forehead. Patton continued the drill for twenty minutes, ignoring the bleeding gash above his eye. His troops admired the show of strong, cool will. Patton was learning his profession well.

Spending the Christmas of 1909 with Bea and

her family, Patton decided that they should make a decision about whether or not to get married. Bea's father was reluctant to see his delicate daughter marry a soldier. He was also concerned that Patton would not have enough money to support her, so he asked Patton for a financial statement. Receiving the statement from his father, Patton was surprised to see how much he was worth, and proudly presented it to Mr. Ayer. When he saw that Patton couldn't be intimidated, he gave the couple his blessings.

On May 26, 1910, all the Boston newspapers covered the wedding. At the grand social affair, Bea married Lieutenant Patton in Beverly Farms' Episcopal Church, near Pride's Crossing, Massachusetts. The ushers, all military men in full dress uniform, drew their sabers and formed an arch as the newlyweds left the small, gothic chapel.

After spending a month-long honeymoon in Europe, Patton returned with his bride to Fort Sheridan to a cramped duplex house with old, thin walls. The duplex was a humble beginning for the couple, but it was the only house available at the time.

Bea made a surprisingly quick adjustment to army life—and an army husband. She softened his rough manner by soothing his temper and his pride, and teaching him the art of flattery. She was also an immediate boost to Patton's career. Because of her fluency in French, she could help her husband translate French cavalry manuals into readable English. The secretary of war's advisory committee, the General Staff, published them, and Patton's name circulated among the brass (high-ranking officers). Bea's dedication to her husband's future created a lasting bond between them.

In March 1911, Bea gave birth to a daughter, Beatrice, Jr. Much of Bea's time was devoted to the baby's care, and Patton felt neglected. He bought a typewriter and started writing articles on military subjects.

Phrases such as "push forward, attack again, until the end," and "blow follows blow" filled his articles. Patton quickly became known for his strong recommendation of offensive (attacking) warfare.

After almost two years at Fort Sheridan, Patton was eager for a transfer. He felt he had learned all he could at the small outpost. Using his family's influence, he asked for a transfer to the army chief of staff headquarters at Fort Myer in Washington, D.C. At Fort Myer, high-ranking officers played polo on manicured fields, and exclusive clubs entertained "all the big men." Patton said Washington, D.C., was "nearer God than elsewhere and the place where all people with aspirations should attempt to dwell."

At his new post, Patton bought thoroughbred horses for racing and shows and dined where the brass gathered. He performed his duties with enthusiasm, determined to step out of the anonymous ranks of second lieutenants. His hard work and athletic zest were rewarded in 1912 when he was appointed the army's representative for the Modern Pentathlon in the Fifth Olympic Games at Stockholm, Sweden. In June, George Patton, and his wife, mother, father, and sister boarded the steamship *Finland* and set off for Europe.

Patton, a skilled athlete, was well prepared for the competition. The pentathlon tested the fitness of the military man and included pistol shooting, swimming, fencing, horse races, and cross-country races.

Plunging into the games with his usual energy, Patton, the only American in the competition, finished fifth overall out of forty-two contestants. He was especially proud of being the only fencer to beat the French champion. When Patton discovered that a French army staff officer, Adjutant Cléry, was the best swordsman in Europe, he was eager to work with him to sharpen his fencing skills. Because he

George Patton practices hurdles for the 1912 Olympics.

was so close to France, he decided to take the opportunity to go to the French cavalry school in Saumur where Cléry was teaching. For two weeks, the ringing clash of Patton's sword echoed through the galleries. Cléry helped Patton polish his footwork, timing, thrusts, and parries while Bea helped Patton with his French.

When Patton returned to Fort Myer in September, he used his newly mastered skills with the saber to write a special report on its handling. His articles were very well received among the senior officers of the War Department. In December, he was assigned temporarily to the Office of the Chief of Staff and was directed to design a new saber. The new weapon, designated "U.S. Saber, M 1913," was better known as the "Patton Sword." Patton redesigned the saber to make it a weapon of attack by lengthening and straightening the curved blade. He also added a larger, protective handle. The cavalry continued to use the sword for the next four years.

In 1913, Patton and Bea sailed back to France, so Patton could study under Cléry once more to perfect his fencing techniques and learn Cléry's methods of instruction. This training would prepare him to teach fencing at the Mounted Service School in Fort Riley, Kansas, as the army's first Master of the Sword. At the school, Patton would

Second Lieutenant George Patton tests his skills with the saber in 1913.

also take the cavalry course. He would be both teacher and student.

On this lonely, dusty post in Kansas, Patton's military reputation for mastery and perfection climbed. Although superior officers regarded him with affection and respect, Patton still doubted his abilities. In November, on his birthday, Patton wrote a gloomy passage to his father: "I certainly am aging...I fixed twenty-seven as the age when I should be a brigadier [general], and now I am twenty-nine and not a first lieutenant."

Chapter/Five

Getting into a Fight

In February 1915, Bea gave birth to another girl. Bea named her Ruth Ellen, despite the fact that Patton wanted to name the baby "Bea II."

Four months after Ruth Ellen was born, Patton graduated from the Mounted Service School, and was transferred to the Eighth Cavalry at Fort Bliss in El Paso, Texas. This was the assignment Patton had hoped for. Mexico had been in a revolution since 1910, and different Mexican groups were violently competing for power. President Woodrow Wilson had stationed troops along the border to prevent Mexican bandits from entering the United States. Fort Bliss was headquarters to Brigadier General John J. "Black Jack" Pershing, who commanded the brigade for the army's protective mission.

Patton prayed for action.

Not long after the Patton family had settled in El Paso, Patton was sent for border patrol ninety miles southeast to Sierra Blanca, a scrubby Texas frontier town nestled in the high country. Consisting of about twenty houses and a saloon, the isolated little town seemed lost in time. Men strutted around in boots and spurs with six-shooters strapped to their hips. The Wild West atmosphere and colorful characters fascinated Patton.

For five months, Patton wandered the wild, rugged mountains, patrolling the ranches around Sierra Blanca. It became a boring job, so he amused himself by shooting any wild game that crossed his path.

Comical episodes also helped to break the tension. Once, from the top of a ridge, Patton spotted a column of dust four miles long. Convinced it was an army of Mexican rebels, he snapped off orders to his men and rode furiously down the slope—only to capture a herd of shuffling cattle.

Although most of the border patrol alarms were false, the danger of a Mexican attack was real. On March 9, 1916, Francisco "Pancho" Villa led several hundred Mexican bandits across the border, raiding Columbus, New Mexico. They burned buildings, killed seventeen Americans, and then fled back over the border into Mexico. General Pershing was ordered to lead an expedition into Mexico and capture Villa.

Upon returning to El Paso, Patton heard his regiment was not going on the expedition. However, he soon discovered that one of Pershing's regular aides was absent and immediately bombarded his superiors with requests for a transfer to Pershing's staff.

Later, Pershing called Patton. "Everyone wants to go," he said. "Why should I favor you?"

"Because," answered Patton, "I want to go more than anyone else."

Impressed with Patton's eagerness, Pershing took him on as an aide. Patton's sister, Nita, may have improved his chances of going, too—she was dating Pershing at the time.

The first few weeks in Mexico seemed glamorous and exciting. Columns of troops totaling fifteen thousand men traveled four hundred miles through the mountains of northern Mexico. As Pershing's aide, Patton attended to his commander's minor tasks, but the excitement faded quickly. Pursuing Villa was next to impossible, since Villa did not want to be found and knew the countryside well.

In May, six weeks into the campaign, Patton heard that Julio Cárdenas, Villa's head bodyguard, lived nearby, either in the hamlet of Saltillo or in

San Miguelito. Accompanied by a group of soldiers, Patton rode to the ranch at Saltillo, searched it, and found nothing. At San Miguelito, he found Cárdenas's uncle, wife, and baby, but not Cárdenas.

On May 14, Pershing sent Patton out to the surrounding farms to buy corn for headquarters. He took fourteen men in three Dodge touring cars. During the course of the errand, Patton began to suspect that Cárdenas was in the area. He decided to return to Saltillo to investigate.

When he and his men neared the ranch, Patton sped up, zoomed past the house, then skidded to a stop. At that same time, the other cars halted at strategic points. Armed with his ivory-handled pistol and a rifle, Patton hopped from the car and ran to the large, arched gate leading to the house's patio. The other men surrounded the house.

Suddenly, three armed men on horseback charged past Patton and through the front gate. He held his fire, remembering Pershing's orders to shoot only in self-defense. The riders turned away when they saw Patton, only to find more soldiers rushing toward them. The horsemen wheeled back around and shot at Patton. As the bullets kicked up gravel around his feet, Patton aimed his revolver and quickly shot five rounds. The soldiers followed suit.

Patton, smoking his pipe, enjoys the rough "cowboy" life in Mexico in 1916.

When the dust settled, all three Mexicans were dead. Patton was thrilled to find that one of them was Cárdenas.

Driving back to headquarters with the corpses strapped on the car hoods, Patton's little convoy caused a commotion as it passed through villages. Pershing was delighted when he heard what happened. He called Patton his "bandit" and promoted him to first lieutenant.

The story made national headlines in U.S. newspapers; the media labeled Patton a hero and called the skirmish "one of the prettiest fights of the campaign." Patton was credited as the world's first officer to use "motorized" military action.

In a letter to Bea and his family, Patton wrote, "I have at last succeeded in getting into a fight."

The expedition continued searching for Villa in early 1917 with poor results; the bandit was never caught. In February Pershing took his men back home to El Paso where they received a rousing welcome.

Working with Pershing had been a valuable opportunity for Patton. He had learned the importance of supply, aerial observation, and proper troop movement. Pershing gave his young aide excellent recommendations and Patton was assigned a troop command at Fort Bliss.

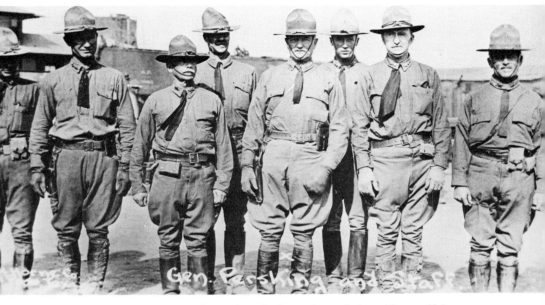

General John J. Pershing (fourth from the right) *and his staff during the expedition in Mexico in 1916. Patton is third from the right.*

This assignment wouldn't last long. On April 6, 1917, the United States declared war on Germany. The Great War, or World War I, had been underway since Archduke Francis Ferdinand of Austria-Hungary was assassinated on June 28, 1914. Austria-Hungary blamed Serbia, its longtime enemy, and declared war. Other European powers were soon drawn into the conflict. When the fighting began, the Allies—France, Great Britain, and Russia—were on Serbia's side against the Central Powers of Austria-Hungary and Germany.

The United States tried to remain neutral, but declared war on the Central Powers after German submarines began to sink unarmed American passenger ships.

Pershing, appointed commander in chief of the American Expeditionary Force (AEF), promoted Patton to captain and put him in charge of the headquarters company to be stationed in Paris, France. Less than two months after returning home from Mexico, Patton said good-bye to Bea and his daughters, and sailed to a world war.

Chapter/Six

Let's Go Get Them!

By mid-1917, Europe was exhausted from three years of bitter war. Millions of men had been slaughtered on the trench-scarred fields of France. National economies strained. When America's large, well-equipped army entered the war on the side of the Allies, the Allied forces breathed a sigh of relief.

In Paris, Patton and Pershing worked hard to set up training facilities for the thousands of incoming American troops. As Pershing's aide, Patton toured the training camps and accompanied him on important meetings with the English and French commanders. Eager for action as usual, Patton wanted to go to the front and lead men in battle. He expressed his frustrations to Pershing, who gave Patton two choices: to be a major in the infantry or in the

newly formed American Tank Corps. This was a
tough decision for Patton, but he decided to risk an
assignment in the tank corps. Because the corps was
still in its early stages, he could have a chance to
become the number-one tank officer. In the infantry, he would only be one among many majors.
When Patton informed Pershing of his decision, he
was sent to France to train at the tank center near
Compiègne.

In France, Patton soon saw that tank develop-
ment had a long way to go. The huge vehicles con-
stantly broke down and had difficulty moving
through rough terrain. The French and the British
argued about how to use the tanks—as giant, protective units to transport troops through enemy
lines, or as movable machine gun and cannon plat-
forms.

At the French tank center, Patton learned everything from attacking with tanks in the field to re-
fueling and repairing them. He visited Cambrai and
other tank battle sites, studying situations where
tanks proved useful and where they failed.

Patton was rapidly becoming the American expert on tank warfare. He was chosen to open and
direct a tank school in Langres, France. Pershing
appointed Colonel Samuel D. Rockenbach as Patton's boss, and together, Patton and Rockenbach

carefully planned the school to prepare it for the arriving tankers.

Just as in his West Point days, Patton instilled unbending discipline in his men. He was "the absolute boss," paying close attention to the smallest of details. Tough training hardened the troops' bodies and minds. The Tank Corps became known as the "Treat 'em Rough" boys.

Patton commanded 250 tankers, but no tanks. Although the machines had been ordered from the United States, production was slow. Finally, the French gave him some of their own Renault tanks. He started field training at once. Rumbling through combat exercises, the tanks advanced side by side to support infantry formations. The First Light Tank Brigade was making progress.

Patton, now a lieutenant colonel, worried that the war might be over before his unit had a chance to fight. Then, Patton's boss, Colonel Rockenbach, sent word that Pershing's First Army was assigned to attack the German defenses around the Saint-Mihiel area in France. A major offensive was set for September 12, and Patton's brigade would be equipped with 144 tanks supporting two infantry divisions.

Patton rushed to obtain ten thousand gallons of gasoline for his tanks and scheduled railroad lines

Lieutenant Colonel Patton at Langres, France, in 1918.

for hauling his units to the front. Battle strategies were planned, and orders were issued. Patton didn't finish until just two hours before the attack. Before his men departed for battle, Patton spoke to his troops: "Finally, this is our big chance: what we have worked for....make it worthwhile."

At 1:00 A.M., nine hundred heavy guns erupted in a dazzling flash along the Allied front; their shells battered the German lines for four hours. A fierce wind blew, and a heavy, pelting rain began to fall. At 5:00 A.M., the soldiers went "over the top."

As the troops advanced toward enemy lines,

Patton stood on a hill to view his tanks' performance, reporting periodically to corps headquarters over the phone. Soon, Patton saw that the tanks were jammed and stalled in the muddy trenches. Determined to get the tanks moving again, he tramped down the hill, and over miles of muddy ground.

Patton urged his men forward. The tanks continued to roll through German towns until they all ran out of gas—except for one. Patton climbed on top of the lone tank to encourage the reluctant driver to keep going. A burst of machine gun bullets, missing Patton by inches, sent him diving into the safety of a shallow hole. Miraculously, Patton escaped the day's fighting without a scratch.

His first battle left him exhausted, but also excited by the furious action. "I at least proved to my own satisfaction that I have nerve," he wrote.

When Patton made his report to Rockenbach, his boss was enraged that he had foolishly endangered his own life and cut the chain of command by running around the battlefield, out of touch with his commanding officer. Patton disagreed with Rockenbach. He believed that he was most needed on the front lines leading his men. Back in the United States, newspaper headlines read, "Californian Perched On Tank During Battle."

Renault tanks of Patton's 304th American tank brigade move to action in the Meuse-Argonne campaign of World War I in September 1918.

Less than two weeks later, Patton's unit was sent sixty miles northwest for an attack in the Meuse-Argonne sector near Verdun. A heavy mist hung in the chilly morning air of September 26. Patton waited in his command post, code-named "Bonehead." As the attack started, Patton's tanks rolled out of sight.

The grinding clash of battle could be heard in the distance, but the fog cloaked Patton's vision. He couldn't stand the suspense. Scrambling forward once again, with a dozen runners, he left Rockenbach's orders unheeded.

Patton and his men soon came under enemy

fire, and again the heavy tanks bogged down in the mud. As a crew quickly tried to dig out the tanks, a German biplane was spotted on the horizon. Deadly shellfire suddenly ripped into the area, and the men dashed for safety.

Patton stood on the trench's edge and ordered his men back to work. He knocked one man's head with a shovel and cursed the rest. When his aides urged him to seek cover, his voice was shrill with excitement. "To hell with them!" he shouted. "They can't hit me!" Ashamed, the men grabbed their shovels and went back to their digging. The tanks, freed at last, gunned up a slope and disappeared over a hill.

Patton returned to the knoll, triumphantly waving his walking stick over his head. "Let's go get them!" he yelled. "Who's with me?"

The men cheered and jumped to their feet to follow Patton's fearless example, charging over the crest in a great rush. Scarlet tracers sliced the air. Machine guns chattered as bullets rained over Patton's men.

Patton tumbled for cover. Overwhelmed, he trembled with fear as he lay flat against the ground. He wanted to run.

A cloud floating above the German lines roused Patton's curiosity. He believed that he saw

the billows form the familiar figures of his fore-
fathers, who appeared to be gazing down disapprov-
ingly. Patton would not let them down. He picked
himself up, drew his pistol, and trudged forward,
waving his stick. "Let's go, let's go!" he yelled.

Only six men followed. Then, one by one, each
soldier slumped in a lifeless heap. Patton's assistant,
Joe Angelo, ran up to his side.

"We are alone," said Angelo.

"Come on anyway," replied Patton.

Just then a bullet tore through Patton's leg. By
sheer will, he struggled on over the broken land-
scape, but fell after a few yards. Angelo dragged
Patton into a shellhole, dressed his wound, and then
hurried back for help. As several tanks rolled by,
Patton directed them toward the German machine
guns, less than forty yards away. When the fighting
slowed down, Patton was loaded on a stretcher and
carried away.

While recovering in the hospital, Patton was
promoted to full colonel. Later, he was awarded the
Distinguished Service Medal and the Distinguished
Service Cross for "conspicuous courage, coolness,
energy, and intelligence in directing the advance of
his brigade."

On November 11, 1918, the day Patton turned
thirty-three, the war ended when the Germans ac-

cepted the armistice (truce) agreement proposed by the Allies. World War I had devastated Europe. Nearly ten million soldiers died in the war, and about twenty-one million were wounded. Armies had destroyed villages, farms, factories, and bridges. Trenches and shellfire had torn up the countryside.

Patton was truly sorry to see the war end. He wrote in his diary, "The end of a perfect war. Fini."

Chapter/Seven

Life Has Lost Its Zest

On March 2, 1919, George Patton boarded the SS *Patria* and sailed home. Patton and his men were greeted as heroes. Marching bands, reporters, and important officials crowded the docks of New York, awaiting the arrival of the Tank Corps. For Patton, however, the glory wore off quickly.

One evening, in Washington, D.C., Patton turned his car into a driveway and stopped in front of a stately house where he and Bea were attending a formal dinner party. Patton's crisp dress uniform glimmered with medals as he escorted his wife into the foyer.

Someone sitting nearby muttered an insult.

Bea walked over to him. "What did you say?" she asked.

"I said that man's one of those all chicken," he said, pointing to Patton's "bird" colonel emblem on his uniform. "Chicken on the shoulder and chicken in the heart."

Bea was furious—she felt her husband's frustration as much as he did. Postwar America had no need for a strong army, much less Patton's "death-defying courage." Patton was frustrated with the attitude of the U.S. government toward the military—especially the Tank Corps. Rumors circulated that the corps would be dissolved completely.

After some long talks, Patton and his close friend, Lieutenant Colonel Dwight D. Eisenhower, decided to leave the Tank Corps and return to their old army outfits. Patton gave up his colonel rank to be a captain in the cavalry. Soon he was promoted to major and transferred to Fort Myer. His next few years were marked by a series of staff jobs and a busy social life. Polo, racing, hunting, and showing horses served as outlets for his pent-up energy.

As Patton's social life grew, so did his family. Patton was thirty-eight when Bea had a son on Christmas Eve of 1923. Following tradition, they named the baby George Smith Patton. The proud father had high hopes for his son—perhaps he, too, would carry out the Patton legacy with honor and pride.

At the time little George was born, Bea and the family were in Massachusetts, and Patton was attending the Command and General Staff College in Kansas. When he was later transferred to the Schofield Barracks in Hawaii, Bea and the children joined him.

In Hawaii, Patton was the director of army intelligence operations. Although this position pleased him, he continued to feel restless. When his parents came to visit the tropical islands, Patton told his father that wars were scarce, and that he felt as if time were wasting away. His father replied that the biggest war in history was just around the corner, and George was being prepared for some special work. The last words George heard his father say were, "Good-bye, old man. Take care of yourself."

The elder Patton died the next year, while George was still in Hawaii. Arriving too late for the funeral, he went alone to the grave in the San Gabriel churchyard. George stood there for an hour, cap in hand, deep in thought. He looked up, and for a moment, he sensed that he had seen his father bundled up in his checked overcoat and waving his stick.

"I knelt and kissed the ground, then put on my cap and saluted, not Papa, but the last resting place of that beautiful body I had loved." Later, Patton

Patton enjoys his leisure time fishing and boating in Honolulu, Hawaii, in 1926.

wrote, "Oh! darling Papa. I never called you that in life…but you were, and are my darling. I never did much for you, and you did all for me."

Patton returned to Hawaii as director of plans and training. One year after his father's death, George's mother died.

In 1928, Patton returned to Washington, D.C., as a staff member in the Office of the Chief of Cavalry. Later, he attended the highest educational institution in the army: the War College. The commandant of the college called him an "untiring student" who was "superior" in all classifications.

Finally, after years of staff jobs, Patton was assigned as executive officer of the Third Cavalry Regiment at his old Virginia stomping ground of Fort Myer. Soon after his new assignment began, Patton was faced with an unpleasant task.

In 1932, twenty thousand World War I veterans came to Washington, D.C., demanding a bonus that the government had promised to pay them at a later date. The country was experiencing the economic disaster of the Great Depression, and many veterans were poor, hungry, and desperate. Although there was little violence at this stage of the "Bonus March," President Herbert Hoover and Army Chief of Staff Douglas MacArthur feared a riot might develop.

Hoover called on the army to rid Washington of the marchers, and Patton's Third Cavalry was among the army troops assigned to the task. Patton led his men across the Memorial Bridge and waited for the infantry on the Ellipse behind the White House. He rode alone down Pennsylvania Avenue to check the streets. Thousands of veterans who recognized Patton from World War I greeted him with a combination of cheers and curses. Assuming his stiff, icy "war face," Patton went as far as Third Street, and then returned to the Ellipse.

When the infantry arrived, MacArthur issued orders to move down Pennsylvania Avenue in assault formation. The army charged into the horde of veterans under a shower of bricks and a fog of tear gas. Patton nudged his skittish horse forward, herding the mob back, and whacking the marchers with the flat of his saber.

The veterans were soon pushed out of Washington, but the Bonus March episode disturbed the United States Army for years. Patton didn't like the idea of marching against ex-U.S. Army men, but he was a soldier, and he followed orders.

In May 1935, Patton, again a lieutenant colonel, was sent back to Hawaii. A self-taught sailor, he bought a fifty-two-foot schooner, the *Arcturus*, and launched it from the California coast for a month's sail to Honolulu. Bea and some close friends served as crew.

Patton was glad to be back on the islands again, but he wasn't looking forward to another office job. Assigned as the director of the intelligence department at Fort Shafter, his job was to strengthen Hawaii's internal security in the event of a war with Japan.

Japan had recently conquered Manchuria, a rich and fertile region of China. The nation's speedy conquests in China threatened American interests in the Far East. After careful study, Patton concluded that Hawaii was also vulnerable to sea and air attack from Japan. He submitted warning reports to his superior officers that were soon filed and forgotten.

By this time, Patton was fifty years old, balding, and near-sighted. He had gained weight, and wore a partial denture in his mouth. Yet he still possessed his boyish pep and vigor, and often felt like a nervous race horse penned in a tiny stall. Sometimes, he flared into fits of anger which were followed by periods of depression. Bitter and frustrated, he realized that his army career wasn't going anywhere. Life had "lost its zest" for him.

The Patton home was not always happy. Bea and the children bore the brunt of Patton's rage and frustration. Bea, however, still tried to cool his heated temper.

Patton's stay in Hawaii ended in the summer of 1937. Bea and George Patton, and their son George, boarded the *Arcturus* with a crew of friends for the voyage back to California and to Massachusetts.

One day, while riding with Bea at their country estate in Hamilton, Massachusetts, a horse kicked and fractured Patton's leg. When a clot formed in his bloodstream, he came close to dying. Patton's army career looked bleak as he lay in the hospital for more than three months.

Although Patton was slightly disabled and wore an iron leg brace, medical officers assigned him to limited duty at the Cavalry School at Fort Riley early in 1938. Stubbornly exercising his leg, he regained full strength. War was brewing in Europe and Patton did not want to miss it.

Chapter/Eight

Old Blood and Guts

Ever since World War I, Europe had remained weak and unstable. Forceful leaders in the Soviet Union, Italy, and Germany were taking advantage of the weakened condition of many European nations to expand their territories and gain power. These dictators terrorized anyone who opposed their rule.

The Nazi party in Germany, led by Adolf Hitler, vowed to avenge Germany's defeat in World War I. Hitler built up the German military forces at a rapid rate. Soon, Germany, Italy, and Japan had joined together in a military alliance.

Wary of the world's instability, the U.S. government released more money for the U.S. military and increased the number of troops. The army promoted Patton to full colonel, and transferred him to command a regiment of the First Cavalry Division at Fort Clark, Texas.

Patton preferred the power of command to the dull paper shuffle of a boring staff job. His fighting speeches to his men caught the interest of the media. He told the training soldiers that they could benefit from seeing some "blood and guts." The newspapers picked up the term, and Patton became known as "Old Blood and Guts."

Patton staged mounted troop maneuvers whenever possible; he loved being back in the saddle. Just as he was beginning to enjoy himself, a phone call informed him of new orders. To his dismay, he was being sent back to Washington, D.C., in December. The move, however, would be Patton's first step toward the next world war.

On September 1, 1939, Germany invaded Poland, causing France and Great Britain to declare war on Germany. By the summer of 1940, German *Panzer* (tank) units had crushed the Polish cavalry, roared into France, and chased the British army off the continent and into the sea. World War II had begun. The Allies, France and Great Britain, were fighting against the Axis Powers of Germany, Italy, and Japan.

U.S. Army Chief of Staff George C. Marshall watched Nazism sweep across Europe. Alarmed by

Colonel Patton and his staff at Fort Myer in June 1940.

the swiftness of Hitler's *blitzkrieg* (lightning war), he rushed to test his own army's strength against such an enemy.

Marshall sent Patton to referee military maneuvers in Texas which would test tank warfare against the horses in the cavalry. When the tanks outperformed the horses, Marshall immediately ordered the creation of two armored divisions: one at Fort Knox, Kentucky, and the other at Fort Benning, Georgia.

In the summer of 1940, Patton tearfully left the cavalry and assumed command of the Second Armored Brigade at Fort Benning. After twenty frustrating years, he was a tanker once again.

Patton enthusiastically shaped the brigade into prime fighting condition. He lectured his officers with inspiring speeches that overflowed with profanity, and his spirited charm enchanted the men. They felt privileged as members of Patton's team. During this time, Patton was promoted twice: first to brigadier general, then to major general.

Patton's men called themselves "blitz troopers" and nicknamed their division "Hell on Wheels." The power of tanks was proved many times in war games staged in Tennessee, Louisiana, and Texas. "All that is now needed," Patton wrote a friend, "is a nice juicy war."

Major General Patton on "war game" maneuvers in Louisiana.

On December 7, 1941, the Japanese attacked Pearl Harbor in Hawaii. The United States declared war on Japan, and Germany and Italy then declared war on the United States. Patton's hopes of war were now a reality.

In July 1942, Patton was summoned to Washington to plan for Operation Torch, the Allied invasion of North Africa at Morocco.

From France to the Soviet Union, from the Arctic Circle to Africa, the Nazi armies had conquered vast territories. The Allies were determined to block the Nazi forces, and they had a plan. The British and Americans would invade North Africa from two sides and trap Hitler's *Afrika Korps.*

Marshall ordered Patton to command the First Armored Corps, and then sent him to train in the desert areas of California, Nevada, and Arizona. This wasteland resembled the terrain of North Africa. The troops called it "the place that God forgot" because the land of sand, rock, and mountains was empty and desolate. Rattlesnakes and coyotes were the only living creatures in sight.

Patton had little time to organize his part of the operation. He worked at a breakneck pace, attending to every detail. Finally, Patton and his troops boarded transport ships and set out to cross the Atlantic on October 24.

After crossing a stormy ocean, the one hundred ships of Patton's Western Task Force lay anchored in smooth waters off the Moroccan coast, cloaked in the night's darkness. It was 2:00 A.M., November 8, 1942. Aboard the flagship cruiser *Augusta*, General Patton stepped on deck to see the lights of Casablanca glitter on the black, glassy water.

During the two-week voyage, Patton wrote in his diary, "...my whole life has been pointed to this moment. When the job is done...I will be pointed to the next step in the ladder of destiny...all I want to do right now is my full duty."

Hundreds of miles northeast, two other task forces prepared for the North African invasion, landing in Algeria at Oran and Algiers. Patton's friend Eisenhower, now the supreme commander of Allied forces, was in charge of Operation Torch and responsible for all task forces involved.

Patton was worried about the upcoming invasion, and did some "extra praying." Morocco was a French colony, but France had been conquered by Germany. Patton did not know whether the French soldiers in Morocco would attack or assist his troops. He was also concerned that the waves off the Moroccan coast would be high enough to capsize his landing crafts at the scheduled invasion time.

Patton had planned for a three-point landing around Casablanca, and the attack was already in motion. From the transport ships, men laden with equipment climbed down webbed netting into the landing crafts and set out for shore before dawn.

It was still dark when Patton heard small arms fire popping in the distance. Searchlights from Pont Blondin and Cape Fédala probed the black sky.

With dawn came a deafening blast.

American warships belched flames from sixteen-inch guns. Airplanes from aircraft carriers hummed overhead, flying for inland targets. French cruisers and destroyers cut through a smoke screen and opened fire on the American fleet. The Americans blasted their reply with accurate aim. Patton stayed on deck as a confusing naval battle churned the oily waters, filling the air with stench and noise.

The beach was in chaos. Instead of setting up aid stations and signal posts, Patton's men were digging foxholes to hide from the incoming shell fire.

With the French fleet crippled and drifting back into their harbors, Patton strapped his pistols to his side, left the ship, and landed on shore, furious with his troops. Shouting and cursing, Patton uprooted groups of men and set them to work. He kicked a crouching soldier to get him moving. He directed men to salvage floundering landing crafts. Order was restored.

After three days of fighting, Patton planned to crush Casablanca with an all-out assault. He set the time for 7:30 A.M. on November 11, his fifty-seventh birthday. Then, less than an hour before the attack, the French asked for a cease-fire.

The Allies were now the occupying force in Morocco, and Patton turned Casablanca into a training base to receive new soldiers and equipment from the United States. Patton was restless and bored in this position; he wanted to be in Tunisia where Eisenhower was pushing east with the Allied forces that had landed in Algeria. By December, the Allied advance in Tunisia had slowed down because of winter rains and tough German resistance.

Then, in February 1943, the German *Panzer* units of Hitler's *Afrika Korps*, led by General Erwin Rommel, struck at the Second U.S. Army Corps at Kasserine Pass in northern Tunisia. The inexperienced Americans pulled back after a number of units were overrun, and finally managed to keep Rommel from reaching their vital supply depot in Tébessa. Kasserine Pass was a military disaster.

The badly mauled Second Corps suffered from low morale and poor discipline. Eisenhower called in Patton and gave him ten days to sharpen the corps into an efficient fighting unit. "For such a job," wrote Eisenhower, "Patton had no superior in the Army."

On the morning of March 6, Patton arrived at the Second Corps headquarters leading a convoy of siren-screeching armored scout vehicles. Confronting tattered, unshaven, and dirty soldiers, Patton jolted the lazy corps with a stream of disciplinary orders. All troops—even doctors, mechanics, and cooks—had to wear helmets, neckties, and leggings at all times. Military courtesy and saluting were strictly enforced, and officers and soldiers fell under stiff fines unless they conformed to regulation.

Patton boosted morale by bringing in new equipment and clothes. Mail became a high priority. He fed his men the best food available, and rushed

Patton, commander of the Second Corps in 1943, looks over the dry landscapes of Tunisia.

hot food even to the frontline troops. Since Patton's corps was going to attack in a matter of days, he fired them up with hard words and vulgar jokes, exciting them for battle.

On March 12, Patton was promoted to three-star general. Captain Dick Jenson, Patton's aide, came to bring Patton a small flag with three white stars on it. That night, Patton slept under the American flag.

Recalling his childhood when he called himself "George S. Patton, Jr., Lieutenant General," Patton wrote, "At that time I did not know there were full generals. Now I want, and will get, four stars."

Eisenhower sent Major General Omar Bradley to be his "eyes and ears" at the Second Corps headquarters. George didn't like the idea of having a spy around, so he made Bradley his deputy commander.

During the night of March 16, the Second Corps attacked the German lines in Tunisia. Allied tanks rumbled through the desert valley floors toward the German and Italian troops. The Germans responded with a heavily armored counterattack that the American First Infantry Division stopped cold at El Guettar. The successful operation caused a sensation back in the United States. Patton was an overnight hero, but he preferred to give his men the praise. The troops had proved to their doubting allies, the British, that they could hold their own against the battle-hardened Germans.

Still pushing his attack to the east, Patton tried to wedge the Germans between his soldiers and the sea, cutting off their escape to Italy. Just as he was gaining speed, his superiors ordered him to stop.

Patton was confused. Why, when he had the Germans on the run, did the brass order him to stop? The answer would never make sense to him.

Chapter/Nine

A Horse Race

In Tunisia, Patton discovered a new enemy—his British allies.

The British Eighth Army under General Bernard L. Montgomery was pushing the Germans from the south when the Second Corps was ordered to stop its advance.

Montgomery, or "Monty," was much like Patton: arrogant, vain, and hungry for fame. He wanted the British to have the glory of beating the Germans themselves, so he tried to persuade his superior, British General Harold Alexander, to limit the Americans' progress.

Eisenhower, as supreme commander, had the difficult job of blending the different Allied troops into an efficient fighting force, and sometimes favored Montgomery's proposals. This, to Patton, was disgraceful. "Ike [Eisenhower]," Patton wrote in his diary, "is more British than the British and is putty in their hands."

Complaining bitterly, Patton convinced Eisenhower to give the Second Corps a more active role in the fighting. Then, on April 15, Patton left Bradley to command the Second Corps for the rest of the Tunisian campaign, and returned to Morocco to plan for Operation Husky—the invasion of Sicily, an island off the coast of Italy.

Husky called for an attack by two armies: the U.S. Seventh Army, commanded by Patton, and the British Eighth Army, commanded by Montgomery. Alexander would command the combined army groups, and Eisenhower was still the supreme commander.

Sicily is shaped like a triangle with points to the south, east, and west. Patton suggested landing his ninety thousand troops in Palermo, on the northwest side, while Montgomery landed in Syracuse, near the southeastern tip of the island. Both forces would then thrust toward Messina on the northeastern shore. This plan suited Patton. He intended to race Montgomery for the prize city of Messina, and be the first to take it.

Montgomery, however, had a different idea for

the invasion—an idea that Eisenhower chose over Patton's. The British army would land at Syracuse, and Patton's army would land along a broad front on the southwestern shores around Gela. Then, while Montgomery plodded toward Messina, Patton would protect the British troops.

Patton's temper flared. The Americans would again play a secondary role to the British. Not only that, his forces would be thinly scattered along the shores, and supplies could only be shipped in from the tiny port of Gela. Montgomery would have the advantage of a narrower front and the major port of Syracuse. Patton's opinion of Eisenhower was sinking rapidly.

Strong winds and rough waves hampered the Seventh Army's landing in the early morning darkness of July 10. Days of fighting passed before the Allied troops established a hold on the shoreline, and naval guns drove back counterattacks from the German and Italian soldiers. Then, Patton quickly pushed north to Messina as planned.

Montgomery had taken Syracuse, and had also started moving north to Messina. After a few days, his forces slowed to a crawl along the east coast road at Catania, blocked at a mountain pass by German soldiers. In order to get around them, Montgomery used a road reserved for Patton's army.

Patton stands by to watch Italian prisoners march through the streets of Palermo, Sicily, in 1943.

Patton had taken enough from Montgomery. He left Bradley's Second Corps to protect Montgomery's troops, formed a Provisional Corps, and struck out on his own toward Palermo. Cutting north, he covered one hundred miles in four days and suffered only three hundred casualties while capturing more than fifty thousand Axis prisoners. Patton seized Palermo on July 22; about the same time, Bradley reached the northern shore of Sicily.

On July 25, Patton met with Alexander and Montgomery to discuss the rest of the campaign. After securing the northern coastal roads for his army, he went to work with renewed energy.

Patton takes the time to chat with a soldier near Messina.

Because Patton was determined to prove the power and skill of his troops, he became obsessed with the capture of Messina. He pushed his officers to move as fast and far as possible to beat Montgomery to the city. As they proceeded along the northern shore, the Germans and Italians dug into the mountains. Patton began losing men rapidly, and by the end of July, his army had ground to a halt.

Still, Patton would not be stopped. "This is a horse race," he said, "in which the prestige of the U.S. Army is at stake. We must take Messina before the British."

Against the strong objections of Bradley and other generals, he ordered a series of complex amphibious maneuvers (sea-to-shore troop landings). On the morning of August 17, thirty-eight days after the Gela landings, forward elements of Patton's Third Division entered Messina. The Germans had already abandoned the city. Minutes later, a British officer sped into town in a jeep, hoping to claim the town for "Monty." He was too late.

Patton arrived in Messina as both American and British armies poured into the town. The senior British officer shook Patton's hand and said, "It was a jolly good race. I congratulate you."

Patton was the conquering hero, crowned in glory. For his dramatic actions at Gela, he was awarded his second Distinguished Service Cross. He had covered more land than Montgomery, captured more prisoners, and lost fewer men in the process. He proved his theory that the lightning attack costs fewer lives than a cautious approach to battle. He was now the most senior, and most experienced battle general in the U.S. Army. By all rights, he deserved further advancement.

Patton gave much of the credit to his men. "Your fame shall never die," he told them.

Unknown to him, Patton's own fame had already been tarnished.

During the struggle for Messina, Patton had
been edgy and pushed himself to near exhaustion.
He endlessly toured the front lines, often stopping
at hospitals and aid stations to visit the wounded
and dying soldiers. To Patton, these men were holy.
However, he had no tolerance for soldiers who pre-
tended to be sick just to stay out of the fighting.

Visiting one hospital, Patton asked a soldier
who appeared to be well what was wrong with him.

"I guess I can't take it," the man told Patton.

Patton flew into a fit of rage, striking the soldier
across the face with his gloves, and cursing him as a
coward. Grabbing the man by the collar, Patton
kicked him out of the tent. Later, doctors discovered the man had malaria.

A week later it happened again. Patton entered
a hospital tent, and saw a man sitting on a bed,
shivering and sobbing. Patton asked what the trouble was.

"It's my nerves," cried the soldier.

"Your nerves, hell!" shouted Patton. "You're
just a...damn whimpering coward." Patton slapped
him with his gloves. "I won't have these brave men
see a yellow [belly] sitting here crying."

Patton slapped the soldier again and turned to
the doctor. "Don't admit this yellow [belly], there's
nothing the matter with him."

Patton pays a visit to wounded soldiers on the front.

Turning back to the soldier, Patton said, "You're going back to the front lines. If you don't, I'll stand you up against a wall and have a firing squad kill you. In fact," Patton said as he reached for his pistol, "I ought to shoot you myself!"

As he left, Patton spoke to the doctor again. "I meant what I said about getting that coward out of here. We'll probably have to shoot them sometime anyway, or we'll raise a breed of morons."

The insulted doctor filed a complaint against Patton through the usual channels. The paper came across Bradley's desk. Out of loyalty to his boss, Bradley filed it away in his safe and forgot about it.

But the doctor wasn't going to forget. He sent another report through medical channels to Eisenhower at his headquarters in Algiers. Eisenhower received it on August 16, the last day of the Sicilian campaign.

Eisenhower sent Patton a blistering letter, ordering him to publicly apologize to the doctors, nurses, and soldiers involved and to every division in the Seventh Army. Patton did, and then sent a personal letter of apology to Eisenhower.

When journalists asked Eisenhower about the incident, he told them the truth and asked them not to publicize the story. He couldn't afford to lose his best fighting general over a scandal. The journalists agreed to keep the story quiet for the sake of winning the war.

Patton thought the matter was closed, but months later, a newspaper columnist and radio commentator broadcasted a slanted version of the "slapping incidents" to the American public. The post offices flooded with letters from citizens to members of Congress, calling for Patton's dismissal.

Eisenhower recognized Patton's misconduct, but still insisted that he was the best battle commander in the army, and therefore should not be dismissed. George Patton had "in thousands of cases personally sustained, supported, and encouraged individuals. I believe that General Patton has a great usefulness in any assault where gallantry, drive, and loyalty on the part of the army commander will be essential," he stated.

Although Patton was not dismissed, he certainly realized his disfavor with Eisenhower. After the conquest of Sicily, his Seventh Army was divided and transferred to Mark Clark's Fifth Army to fight in Italy. Eisenhower then took Bradley to England to help him plan for Operation Overlord— the cross-channel European invasion at Normandy, in France. Later, Patton was stunned to hear that Bradley was chosen to lead the U.S. troops into Europe.

Patton was left wondering if he would ever get another combat assignment. Writing to Bea about his uncertain future, Patton wrote, "Personally, I have complete confidence that this is not my end—I feel more and more that I have a mission which is far from completed...."

But in his diary he wrote, "I have to keep working on my belief in destiny, and poor old destiny may have to put in some extra time to get me out of my present slump...[and] keep on floating me down the stream of fate."

Chapter/Ten

Keep Attacking

Disgraced by the slapping incidents, Patton stewed in his depression. He wondered if he would ever fight again. The army, however, still needed Patton. He was one of the most feared officers in the U.S. Army, and if the Germans knew that he was out of the fight, the reputation of the Allied forces might slip. As a result, the army used Patton as a decoy, and sent him on a tour of the Mediterranean, including trips to Palestine, Egypt, Malta, and Corsica.

As Patton inspected military sites and visited castles and pyramids, news of the commander's whereabouts flashed through the German high command. Patton has arrived in Corsica. Will he attack at Marseille or northern Italy?

Patton's tour ended when Eisenhower called

him to England to command the newly formed
Third Army. In England, Patton set up headquarters, trained troops, and assembled his staff. As
he worked furiously to polish the Third Army, his
bull terrier, Willie, a recent gift from a British
officer, followed closely behind him. The dog
snored loudly and cowered under chairs and beds
when shells blasted nearby. But Patton loved his
dog, and the dog loved Patton.

Much to Patton's dismay, he was still in England when the first wave of Allied troops landed
on the French beaches of Normandy on D day,
June 6, 1944—the largest seaborne invasion in history. A month later, Patton was called to action. He
flew over the English Channel to France where he
set up new headquarters in an apple orchard on the
Cherbourg Peninsula.

His arrival was supposed to be kept secret, but
he was greeted at the airport by a cheering crowd of
soldiers. Patton stood in his jeep and delivered a
short speech: "I'm proud to be here to fight beside
you. Now let's...get the hell on to Berlin. And when
we get to Berlin, I am going to personally shoot
[Hitler] just like I would a snake."

Meanwhile, Bradley, now Patton's boss, geared
up for Operation Cobra, a dense air bombardment
along three miles of the front in France to break

Patton and his beloved dog, Willie.

down the German forces. The raid started on July
25. When the enemy was beaten, Bradley's First
Army smashed through German defenses with armored and infantry divisions.

Two days later, Bradley gave Patton temporary
command of the Eighth Corps. Patton gladly took
control of two armored divisions and ran them side
by side, down the road to Avranches. He captured
the town in three days.

Finally, Patton's Third Army was called to action. His brilliant sweep across northern France
astounded U.S. officials as well as the Germans. He
sent armored columns out in four different direc-
tions, rolling across France at a dizzying speed.

Patton's own brand of *blitzkrieg* caused the
Germans to pull back in confusion. In the first two
weeks after the breakout, nine thousand Germans
lay dead, thirty-eight thousand were wounded, and
thirty-one thousand were captured, all at the hands
of Patton's Third Army.

The German commander in chief, Field Marshal Gunther von Kluge, radioed Hitler. "The
whole western front has been ripped open," he said.
He stressed the need to retreat and regroup. Hitler
would not listen. He ordered von Kluge's Seventh
Army to counterattack westward and retake Avranches. Through the efforts of Montgomery's and

Lieutenant General Patton addresses troops of the U.S. Third Army.

Patton's forces, von Kluge's Seventh Army was soon surrounded and destroyed.

Later, while Montgomery's forces fought the Germans in Falaise, Patton sent units east to the Seine River to liberate Paris from German occupation. Patton loved France, and would have welcomed the opportunity to rescue Paris as a hero, marching in the victory parade. Although the press gave Patton's Third Army the credit for the liberation of Paris, other Allied divisions had the honor of marching in the parade. He was disappointed.

Toward the end of August, Patton's troops continued east into old World War I battlefields. German resistance crumbled as his army passed through France and neared the German frontier. The German West Wall, called the Siegfried Line, fortified the border, but it was undefended at the time. This was Patton's chance to enter Germany and end the war.

He planned to crash through the empty concrete forts and strike for the Rhine River, when, on August 31, his armored columns sputtered and stopped. Patton had outrun his supply lines; his tanks were out of gas. He begged Bradley for more fuel, but by the time the gas started flowing again, the Germans had already regrouped and were fighting hard under a new commander.

Patton stubbornly pushed his men to keep moving. They crossed the Meuse River in Belgium, drove for thirty miles to the Moselle River, and besieged the Germans at Metz, "the strongest fortress in the world."

Finally, Patton's troops were forced to stop. The weather was awful, and supplies and ammunition were scarce. To make matters worse, thousands of soldiers were crippled with trenchfoot, a foot disease.

Patton had the go-ahead for a fresh offensive to start on November 8. The rains were still heavy, and rivers and streams flooded. The countryside was a mess of mud. Patton's generals asked him to postpone the attack and wait for better weather when air support would be available. When Patton refused, the generals returned to their units to prepare for the fight.

By mid-December, Patton had planned to smash through the West Wall and head for the Rhine River and Frankfurt in Germany, but his instincts held him back. To his north, the First Army's battle lines were thinly held by new, inexperienced divisions and troops that needed rest. Patton was nervous about the situation, and he ordered his staff to plan to "be in a position to meet whatever happens." The Allied brass, however, disagreed. They no longer felt threatened by German attack.

They were overconfident. On December 16, 1944, the Germans, led by Field Marshal Gerd von Rundstedt, attacked the Americans in the Ardennes forest through a thick morning fog, and caught the untried soldiers of the First Army by surprise. Soon, the Germans broke through the Allied lines. This offensive became known as the Battle of the Bulge because on a map the battleground appeared to have a bulging shape.

When Patton saw Bradley's map of the bulge, he was amazed at the extent of the German gains. They were slicing toward the Meuse River and threatening the Allies' newly acquired Belgian supply port at Antwerp. The next day, Patton and Bradley met with Eisenhower, now a five-star General of the Army. Top commanders and staff officers gloomily discussed the mounting problems of the German attack. Patton was not so easily discouraged. He was convinced that the Germans could be beaten.

Eisenhower turned to Patton. "When can you attack?"

Patton promised a miracle. "On December 22, with three divisions."

The generals stared at Patton in disbelief. What he proposed was a monumental task. Still, Patton felt confident of his abilities. When he expressed his optimism, the mood of the meeting lightened.

Patton immediately went to work, shifting the advance of his army to a battlefront ninety miles to his north. The soldiers worked around the clock and traveled bumper-to-bumper. Ignoring the black-out regulations, they blazed their headlights at night. Engineers wired thousands of miles of new telephone lines. Sixty-two thousand tons of supplies and ammunition were sent to new depots.

Eisenhower, and even Patton's staff, were still skeptical about attacking too soon with a weak force.

"They were full of doubt," wrote Patton. "I seemed always to be the ray of sunshine, and by God, I always am. We can and will win, God helping."

By December 22, as Patton had promised, his Third Corps spearheaded an attack with three divisions toward Bastogne, in Belgium. At Bastogne, the Germans had surrounded the 101st Airborne Division. Patton and his troops set out to rescue them.

Through a dense blizzard, armored columns advanced cautiously over slick roads. Infantry units plowed through snow-covered slopes, dense forests, and deep, rocky gorges. Patton ordered his officers to attack day and night; there was no time for rest.

Eisenhower (left), *Bradley* (center), *and Patton* (right), *meet at Patton's headquarters in Bastogne, Belgium, in February 1945.*

On December 26, after days of tiring, non-stop combat, the siege ended. The Germans' attack stalled and turned into a full-scale retreat. Patton's promised miracle was now fact.

Still, he was not through. "The only way you can win a war is to attack and keep on attacking, and after you have done that, keep attacking some more," he wrote.

The battle cost the Germans more than 250,000 casualties and tons of equipment. By the end of January, the Allies were pushing against the Western Wall along the front, and the Soviets were attacking the Germans from the east. To build up his dwindling ranks, Hitler started drafting sixteen-year-old boys and middle-aged men.

In early February, Eisenhower assigned Montgomery to lead the main Allied force into Germany and seize the Rhine.

Patton, however, refused to be outdone. With restricted supplies, his army hammered the Siegfried Line in horrible weather. Military traffic muddied the roads, and rivers overflowed from winter thaw. Patton stubbornly pushed his commanders through the German frontier. Soon, Patton was able to ferry an infantry division across the Rhine on rafts and assault boats during the night of March 22, 1945, a day ahead of Montgomery.

Four days after slipping across the Rhine, Patton made what he called his only mistake of the European campaign. Patton's daughters had both married West Pointers, and one of his sons-in-law, John Waters, had been captured earlier in the war by the Germans. Since Patton was near the town of Hammelburg, where the prisoner-of-war camp was supposedly holding Waters, he sent a task force sixty miles behind enemy lines to rescue the American prisoners.

The three hundred men, traveling in fifty tanks, motorized assault guns, and jeeps, ran into trouble. Surprised Germans fired on them as they sped down the road. After they crashed through the stockade, thousands of prisoners jumped on the vehicles and others ran for the hills. A guard shot and wounded Waters. Returning back to its lines, the American force was overwhelmed by German tanks, and surrendered.

The raid was a blotch on Patton's record. Many criticized Patton for risking lives for personal reasons, but Bradley did not. He knew that Patton would take the failure as a hard blow.

After the Allies crossed the Rhine, German resistance dissolved. As the Soviets moved across Germany from the east, Allied elements made contact with them. Hitler's Third Reich was losing power rapidly as large numbers of German soldiers surrendered each day.

Patton's Third Army liberated the Ohrdruf Nord and Buchenwald Nazi concentration camps where millions of Jews and other prisoners were brutally degraded and murdered. The camps horrified and depressed Patton.

Berlin, the capital of Germany, remained to be conquered. Patton wanted to get there first to fight, but this did not happen. Patton was also denied permission to attack Prague, in Czechoslovakia, which further upset him. He hated to see the great capitals of Europe go to the Soviet troops.

On April 25, the Soviets surrounded the city of Berlin. Even under fire from the Soviets, Hitler ordered the German soldiers to keep fighting. Days later, Hitler committed suicide, and soon afterward, Germany surrendered to the Allies. The war in Europe was over. The Allies declared May 8, 1945, as V-E (Victory in Europe) Day.

On May 8, Patton, now a full four-star general, issued his casualty report for the Third Army. They had suffered 136,865 killed, wounded, and missing, while inflicting 530,700 casualties on the Germans and taking 956,000 prisoners. Patton's Third Army had become one of the most effective fighting forces in American history.

As the war drew slowly to a close, Patton wrote to Bea, "I feel lower than whale tracks on the bottom of the ocean. I love war....Peace is going to be hell on me. I will probably be a great nuisance."

Chapter/Eleven

Buried in Foreign Soil

Peace in Europe bred complications. Germany was ruined, and the people, scattered from their war-torn homes, were close to starvation. The government and the economy had come to a halt. Patton's army was ordered to take charge of the American occupation zone in the German region of Bavaria. The zone contained not only Patton's half-million troops of the Third Army, but also millions of Germans, many of them homeless.

Patton did not enjoy this task—he was ill-suited for the job of administrator. His staff officers were given extra freedom while Patton took care of troop duties, a more comfortable job. Yet it seemed to him that "...there was nothing more of interest in the world now that the war was over."

Four-star General George Patton.

Though the war had ended in Europe, it was still going on in the Pacific. Japanese forces had rapidly advanced across Southeast Asia and the western Pacific Ocean since the Pearl Harbor attack in 1941. Patton requested a transfer to the Pacific to fight the Japanese with General Douglas MacArthur, supreme commander of the Allied forces in the Far East. His request was refused. MacArthur didn't want someone as "colorful" as Patton to work under him.

Patton was disappointed. He knew that World War II would be his last war, and he wanted to "see it through to the end."

Patton returned to the United States for a visit with his family and a victory tour. The brave general and his Third Army had become famous, and a hero's welcome was awaiting him. In June 1945, he flew to Boston. After his C-54 landed at Bedford Airport, Patton got off the plane and strode across the runway where Bea and his children were waiting. He doffed his helmet and kissed his wife. "Oh," she said, stroking his cheek, "I'm so glad to have you back." Patton then hugged his son, now a West Point cadet, and his daughters.

A million people thronged the twenty-five-mile route into Boston, cheering Patton as he stood in a bright red fire department touring car. The Charles

Crowds of people greet Patton during his triumphant return to the United States in 1945.

River Esplanade spilled over with twenty thousand more people, welcoming the victorious war hero. Later, in Los Angeles, Patton paraded through the streets in an open car as thousands showered him with confetti, shouting their praises. That night at the Coliseum, one hundred thousand people welcomed Patton with an aerial show, a roaring display of tanks, and fireworks. Swearing and weeping, Patton addressed the crowd, and called for the defeat of Japan.

After visiting his parents' grave and the places of his childhood, Patton traveled to Washington, D.C., to visit his daughters and grandchildren. The

Patton meets with his grandchildren in 1945.

night before his return to Germany, while Bea was upstairs packing, Patton gathered his family in the living room. "I am never going to see you again," he said. "I know this. I am going to be buried in foreign soil."

"Oh, Daddy," said one of his daughters, "don't be silly. The war's all over now."

"Yes, I know. But my luck has all run out...I've spent it all. I have not been a good enough man in my life to be killed by a bullet...I don't know how it's going to happen, but I'm going to die over there."

Patton paused. The room was silent. "Promise

Bea, Nita, and Patton (left to right) *in California.*

me one thing," he said. "Let me be buried over there. In God's name don't bring my body home."

His family promised.

Patton felt out of place in the United States, and he was glad to return to Europe. Sitting beside Bavaria's Lake Tegernsee, surrounded by beautiful scenery, he felt comfortable again. The Third Army headquarters was his home.

Patton, however, was quickly becoming overwhelmed by his job as administrator of the American occupation zone in Bavaria. Americans were sick of war, but war was all Patton knew. He wanted the United States to fight another war, this time with the Soviet Union, a U.S. ally in World War II.

To make matters worse, he suggested forming a military alliance with Germany. To the press, he compared the Nazi party to the Democratic and Republican parties in the United States. To a war-weary country that still considered Germany the enemy, Patton's public remarks were outrageous and insensitive. It appeared that he was losing touch with reality.

Eisenhower suggested that Patton transfer to the Fifteenth Army, a headquarters group formed to write and record the history of the war. Patton, fed up with governing, accepted the position, and on October 7, 1945, he boarded a train and left his beloved Third Army. That night, as Patton dined with a friend, he said, "And now, what is there left for me to do? I've obeyed orders and done my best; and now there's nothing left."

His new job with the Fifteenth Army took him on a tour of Europe. He visited Paris, Brussels, Luxembourg, and Copenhagen. City officials honored him with certificates and decorated him with ribbons. In Stockholm, he met surviving members of the 1912 Swedish Olympic team. In November, much of Patton's time was spent writing "Notes on Combat," and he planned to go home for Christmas to discuss his army future with Bea.

He was scheduled to fly to the United States on

Monday, December 10, 1945. The day before his
flight, Patton and his friend, General Hobart "Hap"
Gay, climbed into a chauffeured limousine to hunt
pheasant near Mannheim, Germany. As they ram-
bled down the road, an army truck traveling in the
opposite direction tried to turn left and swerved in
front of the limousine. The two vehicles crashed,
hurling Patton into the driver's partition. His nose
and neck were broken, and he was completely para-
lyzed. No one else in the accident was even bruised.

He joked with the doctors and orderlies as they
checked him into a hospital in Heidelberg. "What a
way to start a leave," he said.

When Eisenhower heard the news, he sent a
plane to the United States to bring Bea and special-
ist Dr. R. Glen Spurling to Germany. The story of
Patton's accident pushed the news of the Nurem-
berg trials of the top Nazi leaders off the front pages.
Letters flooded the hospital, and Bea answered
every one.

Strapped in traction with large hooks inserted
under his cheekbones, Patton asked Spurling for the
truth. "What chance have I to ride a horse again?"

"None," Spurling said.

"In other words," said Patton, "the best that I
could hope for would be semi-invalidism."

"Yes."

Pallbearers carry General George Patton's casket through the station at Luxembourg on the way to the cemetery on December 24, 1945.

Patton sank into depression. He told his nurse he wanted to "forget it all" and go to sleep, but he held on to life for a few more days.

One afternoon Bea was reading to George as he lay quiet and relaxed. "I feel like I can't get my breath," he said suddenly. A doctor rushed in and held an oxygen mask to Patton's face.

The next day, December 21, his pulse was weak. Several times, he told his nurse he was going to die. That afternoon, Bea read to him, and he became drowsy. "It's too dark," he said to Bea. "I mean, too late." Then he fell asleep.

Bea left her husband sleeping and went with Spurling to eat in the hospital dining room. Halfway through the meal, a messenger came in and asked them to come with him. When they entered the room, they found that Patton was dead.

His family kept their promise. Under a low, overcast sky, Patton's body was buried among six thousand fallen soldiers of the Third Army in the American Military Cemetery at Hamm, Luxembourg.

At the head of his grave stands the plain, white cross of an American soldier, inscribed with his name, rank, and serial number.

/ Afterword

George Patton once said, "The only way for a soldier to die is by the last bullet in the last battle of his final war." To Patton, dying on the battlefield as a soldier fighting for his country would be a noble end to a life. As it was, Patton struggled for his life in a hospital bed—"a hell of a way for a soldier to die," he said.

After Patton's death, the public weighed his accomplishments against the controversy he stirred throughout his life. An article in the *New York Times* stated, "History has reached out and embraced General George Patton. His place is secure. He will be ranked in the forefront of America's great military leaders...."

It was George Patton, however, who reached

out and embraced history. In this sense, he fulfilled the destiny about which he often talked:

> You have to turn around and know who [destiny] is when she taps you on the shoulder, because she will. It happens to every man, but damned few times in his life. Then you must decide to follow where she points.
>
> You have to be single-minded, drive only for the one thing on which you have decided. Then you'll find that you'll make some people miserable, those you love and very often yourself. And, if it looks as if you might be getting there, all kinds of people, including some you thought were your loyal friends, will suddenly show up, doing their hypocritical damndest to trip you, blacken you, and break your spirit.

Patton recognized his destiny from the time he was a young boy. His belief in fate and his sense of self-importance flourished through his studies of ancient history. Romantic visions of heroic military figures shaded his vision of life. He was different, and he knew it. This difference makes it hard, if not impossible, to completely understand George Patton: the soldier, the husband, the father, the mystic, the man.

Each person who knew George Patton or who

has written about his life holds a different opinion of him. One thing is sure: he affected history, and so he has affected everyone. Through time, his legend, like Alexander the Great's, Julius Caesar's, and Napoleon's, will become a romantic vision for other young people so they, too, can fashion their own destinies and color the pages of history.

Appendix

Major Events in Patton's Life

1885   George Smith Patton, Jr., is born on November 11

1897   Patton enters Stephen Cutter Clark's School for Boys

1903   Patton enters Virginia Military Institute

1904   Patton enters U.S. Military Academy at West Point

1909   Patton graduates from West Point and is commissioned a second lieutenant; Patton joins Fifteenth Cavalry at Fort Sheridan, Illinois

1910   Patton marries Beatrice Banning Ayer

1911   Patton's first child, Beatrice, Jr., is born; Patton transfers to Fort Myer, in Washington, D.C.

1912	Patton competes in Modern Pentathlon at the Olympic Games in Stockholm, Sweden
1913	Patton studies swordsmanship at Saumur, France
1914	World War I begins; Patton becomes Master of the Sword at Fort Riley
1915	Patton's second child, Ruth Ellen, is born; Patton joins the Eighth Cavalry at Fort Bliss, in Texas
1916	Patton participates in John J. Pershing's expedition in Mexico and is promoted to first lieutenant
1917	The United States enters World War I; Patton promoted to captain and sails for France to organize a tank unit; Patton opens tank school at Langres
1918	Patton promoted to major and then lieutenant colonel; he is then active in the Saint-Mihiel and Meuse-Argonne offensives; Patton promoted to colonel; World War I ends when Germans sign truce with Allies
1919	Patton returns to the United States and regains rank of captain of cavalry

1920	Patton promoted to major and joins Third Cavalry at Fort Myer as commanding officer
1923	Patton's third child, George, Jr., is born; Patton enters the Command and General Staff College
1924	Patton graduates with honors from the Command and General Staff College
1925	Patton assigned to Hawaiian Division
1928	Patton joins Office of the Chief of Cavalry in Washington, D.C.
1932	Patton is a distinguished graduate from the Army War College and joins Third Cavalry at Fort Myer as executive officer; Bonus March occurs in Washington, D.C.
1934	Patton promoted to lieutenant colonel
1935	Patton reassigned to Hawaiian Division
1938	Patton serves as executive officer at Fort Riley; he is promoted to full colonel and takes command of the First Cavalry Division at Fort Clark, Texas; he is then transferred to Fort Myer
1939	World War II begins
1940	Patton assigned as commanding officer of the Second Armored Brigade at Fort Ben-

ning, Georgia; Patton is promoted to brigadier general

1941   Patton promoted to major general and becomes commanding general of Second Armored Division; Japan attacks Pearl Harbor, Hawaii, on December 7; the United States enters World War II

1942   Patton commands First Armored Corps in Operation Torch in North Africa

1943   Patton takes charge of Second Corps; Patton promoted to lieutenant general; Patton commands the Seventh Army in Operation Husky in Sicily

1944   Patton commands the Third Army in Europe; Allied forces defeated in the Battle of the Bulge

1945   Patton promoted to full general; World War II ends in Europe; Patton assigned to command Third Army occupation of Bavaria; he then is transferred to the Fifteenth Army; Patton dies on December 21 and is buried in Hamm, Luxembourg

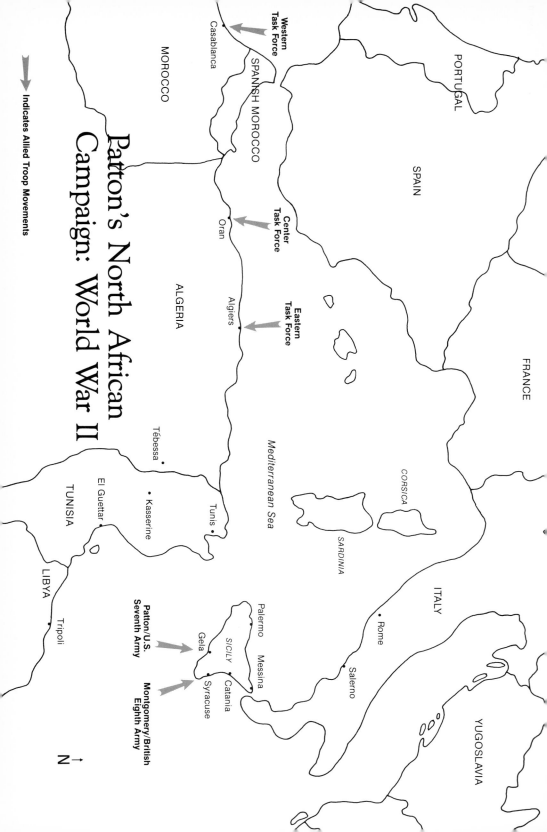

Patton's North African Campaign: World War II

Indicates Allied Troop Movements

PORTUGAL

SPAIN

FRANCE

MOROCCO

SPANISH MOROCCO

Casablanca

Western Task Force

Center Task Force

Oran

ALGERIA

Algiers

Eastern Task Force

Mediterranean Sea

CORSICA

SARDINIA

ITALY

Rome

Salerno

YUGOSLAVIA

Tébessa

El Guettar

Kasserine

Tunis

TUNISIA

LIBYA

Tripoli

Palermo

SICILY

Messina

Gela

Catania

Syracuse

Patton/U.S. Seventh Army

Montgomery/British Eighth Army

N →

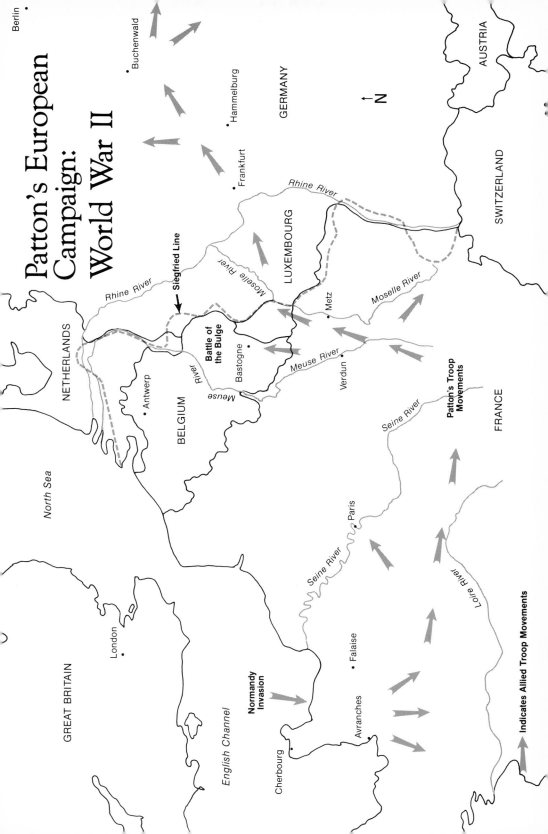

Patton's European Campaign: World War II

Berlin

Buchenwald

Hammelburg

Frankfurt

GERMANY

AUSTRIA

N

Rhine River

Siegfried Line

Rhine River

Moselle River

LUXEMBOURG

SWITZERLAND

NETHERLANDS

Moselle River

Metz

Battle of the Bulge

Bastogne

Meuse River

Verdun

Antwerp

Meuse River

BELGIUM

Seine River

FRANCE

Patton's Troop Movements

North Sea

Seine River

Paris

GREAT BRITAIN

London

Loire River

English Channel

Falaise

Normandy Invasion

Avranches

Cherbourg

Indicates Allied Troop Movements

Selected Bibliography

Ayer, Frederick, Jr. *Before the Colors Fade.* Boston: Houghton Mifflin, 1964.

Blumenson, Martin. *The Patton Papers, Volume I.* Boston: Houghton Mifflin, 1972.

———. *The Patton Papers, Volume II.* Boston: Houghton Mifflin, 1974.

———. *Patton: The Man Behind the Legend 1885-1945.* New York: William Morrow, 1985.

Devaney, John. *"Blood and Guts."* New York: Julian Messner, 1982.

Farago, Ladislas. *Patton, Ordeal and Triumph* (Paper). New York: Dell, 1970.

Mellor, William B. *George Patton, The Last Cavalier.* New York: G.P. Putnam's Sons, 1971.

Patton, George S., Jr. *War As I Knew It* (Paper). New York: Bantam Books, 1980.

Province, Charles M. *The Unknown Patton.* New York: Bonanza Books, 1984.

/ Index